W9-BCJ-432

BORN ON THE CIRCUS

by *Fred Powledge*

☆ ☆ ☆ ☆ ☆ ☆ ☆ ☆ ☆ ☆ ☆

Illustrated with photographs by the author

☆ ☆ ☆ ☆ ☆ ☆ ☆ ☆ ☆

HARCOURT BRACE JOVANOVICH

NEW YORK AND LONDON

Printed in the United States of America

First edition

B C D E F G H I J K

Library of Congress Cataloging in Publication Data
Powledge, Fred.
Born on the circus.
SUMMARY: Describes the hard work and excitement of
circus life as seen through the eyes of an eleven-year-
old who performs as juggler, trampoline artist, and horse-
back rider.
1. Cristiani, Armando—Juvenile literature.
2. Circus—Juvenile literature. [1. Circus—Biography]
I. Title.
GV1811.C74P68   791.3′092′4 [B] [92]   76–2449
ISBN 0–15–209970–0

Photograph on page 36 courtesy of
United Press International

CONTENTS

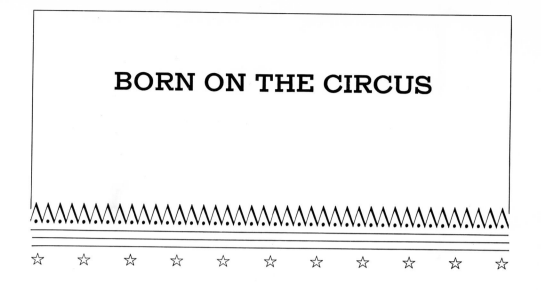

BORN ON THE CIRCUS

The elephants

1

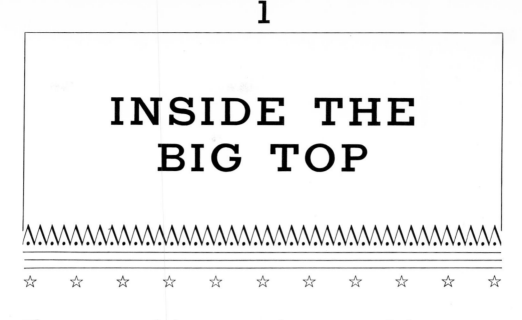

INSIDE THE BIG TOP

The evening rush hour was ending now, and the sun was getting lower in the summer sky. On the circus midway, the lane that forms the main entrance to the big tent, a few people gathered and bought their tickets for the evening's first show. They were the early birds. The loudspeaker on top of the ticket wagon, which had been silent ever since the show had moved in that morning, started playing recorded calliope music.

Behind the sideshow tent, the ten elephants ate their hay. Leo, the man who took care of the elephants, started brushing off the colorful canvas blankets that the animals would wear on their backs when the show started. Near him, the zebras and the llama seemed impatient. Perhaps they knew that it was getting close to show time again.

Johnny Walker, who ran the food joint, looked up at the sun and decided that it was time to put some hot dogs on the grill. Alice Walker, Johnny's wife, started making some fresh popcorn. The circus was coming alive for another day.

Inside the Big Top, which is what the circus people call the main tent, there were very few people. The crowds had not yet gone in, although more and more people were arriving now on the midway. Clarence, an older man who played in the circus band, slowly carried his big drum into the tent and set it up on the bandstand. Some of the circus workers who were called prop men carried colorful platforms and hoops and bunches of feathers into the tent and put them all in the right places. What seemed like hundreds of ropes and cables hung down from the top of the tent. A man and a woman carefully checked the position of a trapeze and the cables that it hung from. They wore bright costumes, but over them they wore bathrobes.

Behind the tent, all the performers had begun stirring. Some of them were finishing their dinners, and some of them were just now really getting awake from afternoon naps. They moved in and out of their trailers, putting on costumes for the first performance of the evening. With some of them, it was difficult to tell from their costumes what sort of performers they were. With others, like the clowns, one knew immediately.

A small boy emerged from a red-and-white trailer. The trailer was longer than most trailers, and it had two horses tied to one end of it. In the middle there were cages holding three leopards. One of the leopards was a baby; the others were big. The small boy, who had bright yellow hair, moved past the leopards without fear. He had on his costume already—red bell-bottom pants and a ruffled white shirt that tied around the waist, like a pirate's shirt.

The boy reached into a bag that was just inside the trailer's rear door, and he produced five wooden rings, each of them covered with brightly colored tape. The rings were about as big around as volleyballs. The boy started juggling the rings in the backyard of the circus. They went higher and higher, and then he dropped one. Quickly he picked it up and started over again.

The boy's name was Armando Cristiani, and he was eleven years old. He was one of the performers in the Hoxie Brothers Circus, and right now he was warming up for his juggling act.

Armando, a member of one of the most famous circus families in history, has been a performer since he was three years old. His parents tell him he is free to be anything he likes when he grows up, but right now he's pretty certain that he wants to continue being a circus performer. He'd *really* like to be a circus star—someone who is very famous and who is known throughout the circus world—but Armando says that's a long way off. Some of his friends and fellow performers, though, say that Armando is being too modest; they say he's a star already.

Armando Cristiani

Now the ticket takers were standing at the front door of the Big Top, and the crowds were going in. This was always an exciting moment in the circus; the people who put on the show were able to see how many people were coming to see them work. Sometimes the circus's local sponsor doesn't do a very good job of selling tickets and getting people interested in the show, and the audience is quite small. That always hurts the performers' morale a little, but they do their best anyway. And, besides, the performers know that the show will be in another town tomorrow—because the circus moves from town to town every day—and that maybe tomorrow's audience will be larger.

Sometimes the local sponsor does a very good job, and the crowds are very large—so large that they more than fill the three thousand seats. When this happens, it's called a *straw house*, because in the old days of circuses the show put down piles of straw for overflow crowds to sit on. Whenever there is a straw house, the performers and other show people feel terrific.

On this particular night in Shelbyville, Indiana, the crowds were large. You could feel the excitement in the air, and Johnny and Alice Walker were having trouble keeping up with the orders for hot dogs.

John Hall, the general manager of the circus, looked at his watch and decided the show should start almost exactly on time—in about fifteen minutes. John was a very tall and quiet man who used to be a schoolteacher until he got hooked on the circus life. He walked through the Big Top and out the back door (which is really just an opening in the canvas) and caught the eye of Phil Chandler. Phil was the ringmaster as well as the magician for the circus, and he had been waiting for John's signal. John nodded his head ever so slightly, and

Phil picked up his whistle, which he wore on a cord around his neck, and blew a blast on it that could be heard all over the backyard. "Fifteen minutes," he yelled. Performers and workmen started moving a little faster, getting ready for the show.

Armando Cristiani checked over his costume. He knew his face was clean and his hair was combed neatly, because he had just left the bathroom in the Cristiani trailer. Just to make sure, he combed his hair again. He stood waiting by the trailer, which was parked close to the back door. All around him performers hurried. Leo brought the elephants up to the back door. The huge gray animals walked slowly, but when an elephant walks, each step covers a great deal of territory.

Phil Chandler blew his whistle again. "Five minutes!" he shouted. Phil had put on his ringmaster's costume, a formal evening suit made out of red fabric. He wore a top hat, and he really looked like a ringmaster. He also really looked like a magician.

Armando ran a few yards from his trailer to the back door of the circus tent. There, next to the entrance, was a stack of flags and banners for the performers to carry when they made their grand entrance into the tent. The first thing that happened in this circus performance, as in many other circuses, was called the *Spec*. That is short for *Spectacular*, and it means the big walk-around that all the performers and many of the animals do to open the show.

Armando picked up his banner—a long stick with a piece of cloth on it, and with paintings of clown faces on the cloth— and he walked over to the back door. All around him performers were getting ready to go into the big tent. Armando's mother, Gilda Cristiani, rode up on her horse. She wore a red, white, and blue cape over her costume. Someone handed Gilda an American flag. Lucio, Armando's father, walked up. He was wearing a clown's outfit and a silly little hat. Then came Tino, who was Armando's fourteen-year-old brother. Tino carried a banner like Armando's.

Then there were the rest of the performers—the McGuire sisters, who had trained doves; the Astros, who rode a motorcycle up a thin cable inside the tent; the trapeze performers; the ponies; the clowns; the zebras and the camel and the llama. Finally, at the end of the line that was forming outside the tent, came the elephants.

Leo walked alongside the elephants, and so did Bert Pettus, who was their trainer. Bert was a man who was getting along in years and who had worked in more circuses than most people had ever heard of. Bert chewed tobacco a lot of the time, and he was always spitting the juice on the ground. He never spat when he was in the Big Top, though; Bert always did only the right things when he was in front of the audience. He was a real showman.

"Line up," shouted Phil Chandler. Everybody was already pretty well lined up, although some of the elephants were trying to wander away to eat some fresh grass they had found. Leo coaxed them back into the line behind the back door. Phil Chandler went inside the tent.

Phil walked to the center of the tent, picked up the microphone, and waited for the crowd to quiet down. It did not take long. Everybody noticed the man in the red formal clothes.

"Children of all ages," said Phil, in a loud and professional voice. "Welcome to this year's edition of Hoxie Brothers three-ring circus." The audience applauded. "And now," said Phil, "on with our show. The theme of our program this year is 'Happiness is a circus parade.' "

Getting ready for the "Spec"

Then the circus band started playing "Happy Days Are Here Again." The back door was thrown open, and Gilda Cristiani entered the Big Top on her horse. The American flag waved in the breeze. Armando was just behind his mother, carrying his banner, and behind him came all the others. They walked around the performing area, just in front of the audience, in a big parade.

As always, the elephants came at the end, but Armando hardly saw them. By the time Bert Pettus and Leo were leading the big animals into the tent, Armando was on his way out. He put his banner down outside the tent, ran to the back door, and started flexing the muscles in his arms and legs. He was getting ready for the first act of the circus, which was the trampoline.

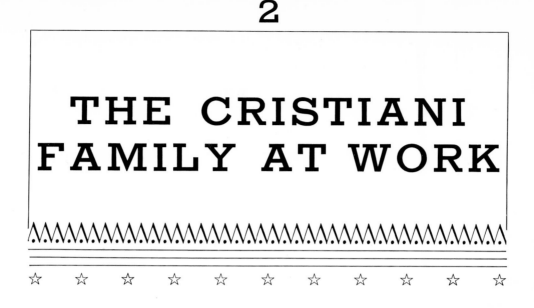

2

THE CRISTIANI FAMILY AT WORK

☆ ☆ ☆ ☆ ☆ ☆ ☆ ☆ ☆ ☆ ☆

Almost everybody has seen a trampoline at some time or other, and a lot of people have bounced on one. Jumping on a trampoline is a lot like jumping on your bed at home, except that you go a lot higher and your parents don't yell at you to stop. There is a metal framework around the outside that holds the trampoline off the ground and holds the center part in place. Elastic cords run from the framework to the center, which is called the *bed*. The bed is very springy.

In the trampoline act, the whole Cristiani family came into the Big Top. Lucio, Tino, and Armando got on the trampoline. Gilda stood on the ground next to it. She did not do any bouncing on it at all, but she still had a very important job: she kept an eye on the rest of the family as they went up and down on the trampoline. If one of them made a mistake and started to bounce the wrong way out of the trampoline, Gilda was there to break his fall before he hit the ground.

First Armando performed on the trampoline, and then Tino got on. Then they performed together. They did somersaults, twists, and flips, and they seemed to be going higher and higher all the time. Then Lucio, who was wearing baggy old clown pants, climbed onto the trampoline. He, too, went higher and higher, until once, when he came down and bounced on the bed, his pants fell down. The crowd roared, because under his baggy pants Lucio was wearing bright red underwear.

The trampoline act: warming up . . .

Tino catches Armando.

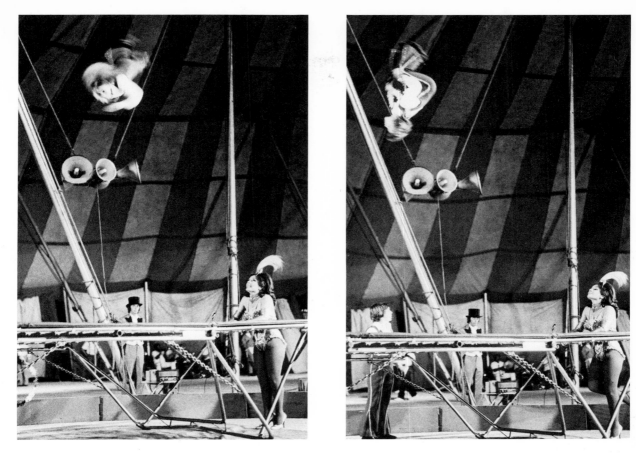

Armando doing flips . . .

He takes a bow.

The three-high

Then the tumbling got serious. The ringmaster announced that the family was about to do a very difficult trick: the "three-high." Lucio stood on the bed. Tino bounced higher and higher, until he finally bounced himself onto Lucio's shoulders. Then Armando started bouncing in front of his father and brother. He had a hoop in his hand. Higher and higher he went, until, after five or six jumps, he did a flip through the hoop and landed with his feet on Tino's shoulders! Suddenly the three Cristiani men were standing there on the trampoline. On top, very high up, holding his arms wide open, was Armando. The trick always brought a big round of applause from the audience.

Then the Cristianis ran from the Big Top to make way for another act—the baby elephants, presented by Bert Pettus. Elephants are extremely intelligent animals, and the circus's six small elephants performed very well even though they were just babies. Like youngsters all over, though, they sometimes liked to go off and do their own thing. Bert was kept busy with them all the time.

After the elephants came what is called the Spanish web. Three of the circus's women performers climbed up thick, heavy ropes that were attached to the roof of the tent, and they turned and twisted and hung upside down in time with the music. It is a tradition in the circus for young women, when they first come to the show, to learn how to do two stunts in particular. One is the Spanish web, and the other is on the aerial ladders—short sections of ladders that swing from ropes, very much like trapezes.

Now it was time for Armando to help his mother with her uncaged-leopard act. The circus workmen put up two heavy pedestals, about four feet high, in the main ring. Then they wheeled the Cristianis' two fully grown leopards into the Big Top in their cages. Gilda carefully opened the cages and brought the leopards out. They were on leashes. Usually, someone in the audience would scream or gasp at this point, because most people are not at all used to seeing wild animals outside some sort of cage.

Gilda talked soothingly to the leopards, and she eased them along until they jumped upon the pedestals. Then, using her whip to guide them (but only rarely hitting them with it, and *never* hitting them hard), Gilda got the animals to stand up on their hind legs. A little later she got the leopards to jump from one pedestal to another.

Then the circus prop men moved the pedestals around until there were three of them in a line. One leopard sat on an end pedestal, and the other one sat in the middle. The leopard on the end jumped into the air, over the other cat, and landed on the empty pedestal.

Lucio came out. He had changed from his baggy clown costume to a dinner jacket and trousers. He took the leash of one of the leopards and coaxed the animal off the pedestal and out close to the crowd. Finally he got the leopard to stand up on her hind legs and walk across the ring. It was a difficult trick to do, because leopards are not used to walking on just two legs. When the trick was completed, Lucio rewarded the cat with a few kind words.

Then Tino brought out another prop and set it between two of the pedestals. It was a large ring resting on a stand. At the bottom of the stand was a container of fuel. Tino turned on the fuel and held a match to the ring. All of a sudden the ring became a circle of fire. Gilda talked to the cat that was on one of the pedestals, and slowly the leopard sank back on her powerful back legs, and then she jumped through the ring of fire to the next pedestal. Gilda rewarded the cat with a kiss.

A little later, the cats climbed up on two other pedestals, which were rounded, like basketballs, and which were covered with tiny mirrors. The pedestals were connected to a motor. The balls started turning slowly, with the leopards on them, while the circus band struck up the music from the movie

Gilda Cristiani and the leopard act

Born Free. The audience always applauded loudly at this, and the uncaged-leopard act was over.

It might sound as if the Cristianis made up the whole circus, and it's true that they did a lot, but they didn't do *everything.* Hoxie Brothers Circus is what is called a *family show,* and that means not only that it's a suitable circus for the average American family to attend, but also that a lot of the performers are members of the same families and that each family does a number of things. It's an old rule on the circus that nobody does just one thing.

While the Cristianis had been doing their trampoline act, another family had been doing stunts on another trampoline in another ring. Now that same family came back and did a clown routine. Then came the girls on the aerial ladders, and after that the trapeze act. The man and woman who had been in the Big Top before, checking their cables, came out and bowed to the audience, and then the man helped the woman climb a rope next to her trapeze. When she got to the bar, which was about twenty feet from the ground, she balanced herself on it and started spinning rings around her arms and legs. Her name was Magaly Rosales, and she and her husband, who stayed on the ground beneath her, were from Mexico.

A little later, Magaly turned herself upside down and stood on her head on the crossbar of the trapeze while she juggled the hoops and rocked the trapeze back and forth. Ruben, her husband, watched her every move because there was no net to catch Magaly if she should fall. Once during the season with Hoxie Brothers Circus Magaly *did* fall from the trapeze. She was taken to the hospital, but fortunately nothing was broken. She had to rest up for several days.

Magaly Rosales on the trapeze . . .

the Astros and their high-wire motorcycle act.

Bert Pettus and the elephants

After the trapeze act came the big elephants. They paraded and waltzed when Bert Pettus told them to, and they ended up in a big line, with each elephant's front legs on the back of the elephant in front. Elephants are big animals anyway, but they seemed especially big now.

Elephants and clowns and trapeze artists are basic parts of any circus, and so is juggling. And that's where Armando Cristiani is the star. He's a fine juggler, and everybody who watches him says that when he gets older he'll be a truly great one.

Now Armando was ready for his act. He stood by the back door waiting for his cue from the ringmaster. "And in ring number one," said Phil Chandler into the microphone, "is the world's youngest juggler—nine-year-old Armando Cristiani." Actually, Armando was eleven, but the circus thought it would sound better to say he was nine. (There is often a bit of exaggeration in show business.)

Armando bowed to the audience. He was smiling, and he had been smiling all the time he was running into the ring. "No matter how bad you might feel, you have to smile," he once said. "You always smile for the audience."

Armando's juggling balls were in his hands. There was a basket of other balls and rings and clubs set up on the other side of the ring. Armando's father stood next to the basket, ready to hand the props to Armando when he needed them.

The circus band started playing a fast tune, and Armando started juggling. He began with three balls, and when he got them going well, he added another, and then another. You could see the concentration on his face as he worked to make sure that all the balls went where they were supposed to go. When he had five balls in the air, some members of the audience applauded Armando.

He dropped a ball. That happens every once in a while. When it does happen, Armando is not ashamed or embarrassed. He knows that things like this happen to every juggler occasionally. He picked up the ball and did the trick again. The audience saw what he had done, and they saw how hard the trick was, and they applauded even more loudly. Armando took a bow. He remembered to smile. In the other two rings, the two other jugglers were taking their bows, too.

Then Lucio handed Armando the rings. Rings, says Armando, are easier to juggle than balls, but they look a lot flashier. Armando had made the rings himself, out of plywood, which he had covered with red, green, and white tape. Those are the colors of the Italian flag. Armando is very proud of being an Italian-American.

Then Armando's father put fuel on some wands and set them afire. He handed them to Armando, and Armando began juggling them, being careful to catch the wands by the ends that were not burning. The effect of the flames—flying through the air over and over again—was very impressive, and the crowd applauded loudly when Armando finished.

Armando bowed deeply, smiling again at the audience. Then he ran out of the ring—straight for the Cristiani family trailer. He changed clothes quickly. The family's final and most important act—the horse-riding act—was only a few minutes away.

Cristianis have been known for dozens of years as excellent bareback riders. There was a time, several years ago, when Lucio and his five brothers would enter the ring and send a horse trotting around in a circle. One of the brothers would stand in the center of the ring, leading the horse around with a whip, and the other five would run and take big jumps and land on the horse's back all at the same time.

Now the Cristiani brothers were all off doing separate things, and the riding act included just one horse and four Cristianis—Lucio, Gilda, Armando, and Tino. But some of the tricks were the same ones that had delighted circus audiences long before Armando was born—back in the 1930s, when the Cristiani family first came to the United States.

Armando juggling the rings

The Cristianis' horse act: Armando, Gilda, and Tino on horseback.

A beautiful white horse galloped around the ring. Tino and Armando took turns running and jumping onto her back. Then Gilda climbed on the horse's back and stood there, without any kind of support, and she danced on the moving animal's back like a beautiful ballerina. It was a very difficult trick to do, especially when the ground was not level. And the ground on a circus lot is hardly ever level. Sometimes there are small holes, which can cause the horse to stumble, and sometimes there are small stones, which can bruise the animal's hoofs. But the Cristianis are famous for their professionalism, and it takes a very bad lot to make them decide not to ride.

Lucio had been missing from the ring while Gilda, Armando, and Tino were riding the horse. Now he made his entrance. But he didn't look like a performer. He wandered around the track in old clothes, looking and acting like a person who has had too much to drink. He shouted that he was a "broncobuster" and that he wanted to ride the horse.

The ringmaster pretended to see Lucio for the first time. He said, "Sir, sir, please get out of here. That's dangerous."

"But I want to ride the horse," pleaded Lucio.

The ringmaster argued with Lucio for a little while, and finally he let him ride the horse. Lucio got on and stood backward on the back of the moving horse. Then he stepped off into thin air, and he landed on the ground all in one piece. By this time, everyone in the audience knew that he was part of the act and was an expert rider.

Lucio then climbed onto the horse's back, and he and the horse went around the ring at breakneck speed, with Lucio looking all the time as if he were about to lose his balance. He pulled off his coat and hat and threw them down into the ring, and Gilda quickly spread out the coat on the ground

Lucio balancing

and put the hat a few feet in front of it. After Lucio went around the ring one or two more times, he leaped off the horse, did two somersaults on the ground, and stood up. While doing the somersaults, he had managed to put his coat and hat back on!

Lucio's next stunt was used to finish the horse act. By this time the crowd was accustomed to seeing Tino and

Armando run across the ring and jump on the moving horse's back, and now it looked as if Lucio were going to do the same thing. The horse went around the ring, faster and faster, and Lucio took a few steps backward and then broke into a run and jumped for the horse's back.

But he didn't land on the horse. His jump took him *over* the horse and out of the ring. Just as he was about to crash into the ground, he curled himself up into a ball and landed on a piece of foam rubber that had been placed just outside the ring. The crowd always screamed when he did this because it looked as if Lucio were going to break his neck.

Lucio accepted his applause, and then he turned and walked back toward the ring. The horse was coming around again now, and as Lucio stepped into the ring he did another somersault, just in front of the horse's flying hoofs. The audience broke into long applause when Lucio stood up unharmed.

The performance was over. Already, on the midway, another crowd was lining up to get into the Big Top for the second performance. For Armando and the rest of the Cristianis, there would be another trampoline act, another leopard act, more juggling, another horse act. And then, Armando thought (and as he thought it his mouth started watering), it would be time for just one thing: dinner.

The horses and leopards and trampoline and juggling balls would be carefully stowed away in the back part of the trailer, and the family would gather in the front part. Everybody would sit down around the small table, and Gilda would put a fine meal on the table—maybe even spaghetti with clam sauce, which was one of Armando's favorites. Armando hoped the second performance would go quickly because he was very, very hungry.

Pisa, Italy

3

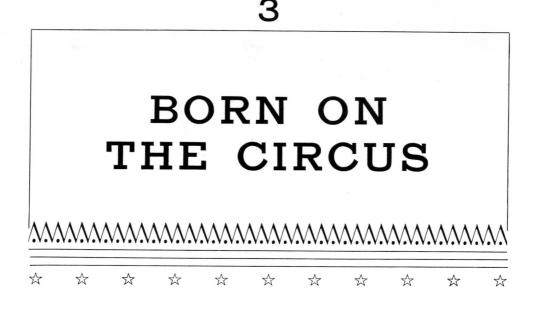

BORN ON
THE CIRCUS

☆   ☆   ☆   ☆   ☆   ☆   ☆   ☆   ☆   ☆   ☆

Armando Cristiani was born in Canton, Ohio, while his family was waiting for a circus to go on the road. He was to become a fifth-generation performing Cristiani.

The Cristianis got into the circus business way back in the last century, in Italy. Armando's great-great-grandfather, Emilio Cristiani, was a blacksmith in the town of Pisa. In his spare time, Emilio liked to invent things, and he liked to do tumbling and gymnastics. He hardly ever thought of doing tumbling for a *living*, though, until after his son, Pilade, was born, in 1852.

Pilade didn't want to be a blacksmith like his father. He liked gymnastics even more than Emilio did, and he enjoyed tumbling in the local gymnasium, and he was a fine weight lifter. Pilade worked as a teacher, but, like a lot of us, he was especially excited on the day when a circus came to town. The people who ran circuses in those days knew that in Pisa there was a young man who was an excellent weight lifter and gymnast, and they often asked Pilade to come to work for the circus on a temporary basis when it was playing in his home town.

On one of those shows that visited Pisa, Pilade met a young woman, Anna Bottari, who was a bareback rider and trapeze performer. They fell in love and got married. Anna's parents, who ran the circus, didn't want their daughter to leave the show, and so they talked Pilade into joining the circus, instead. So when Pilade was eighteen years old, he entered show business on a full-time basis.

Pilade's father, Emilio, the blacksmith, followed his son's fortunes with great interest. It was obvious that Emilio was attracted by the circus business himself. So in 1874 Emilio sold his blacksmith shop, got some money together, and started his own show, with Pilade and Anna. They called it the Cristiani Circus.

Most traveling circuses in those days were family shows, which meant that many of the performers who journeyed from town to town were the brothers, sisters, children, and parents of one big family. Of course, the bigger the family was, the bigger the circus could be. So Pilade and Anna started producing children. After Anna died, Pilade married again, and by the time it was all over Pilade had become the father of twenty-four Cristianis!

Not all of them went into show business. Some became important people in other fields, such as medicine and the law. But quite a few stayed with the circus. One of Pilade's sons, Ernesto, who was born in 1882, was particularly attracted to the life of show business. He became an excellent tumbler himself, and he was good at clowning and working with animals. Ernesto was to became Armando's grandfather.

Ernesto was born into the circus business, and when it came time for him to bring up a family of his own, he did what many circus people do—he married another performer. His wife, Emma Victoria, was a famous trapeze artist. They were married in 1904. Ernesto and Emma did pretty well in the child-raising department, too. They had sixteen children. Because medical care was not so good in those days, six of the children died. The other ten, six boys and four girls, went to work for the family circus. The third oldest son was Lucio Cristiani.

The family, with Ernesto and Emma in charge, traveled all over Europe, delighting audiences and usually making enough money to get by. At first the Cristiani family worked for other circuses, but as the family got bigger, Emma and Ernesto decided that they had enough children to start a show of their own. They traveled all over Italy many times, bringing their circus to small towns and big ones, too.

But then the war clouds of World War II started gathering. Ernesto had been critical of some of the politicians who were running Italy, and he thought it would be wise if the family left its home country. So the Cristianis started working, as a family, for other circuses, in France and England and Germany, always getting better and better and more daring in their performances. In those days, circuses played in one place for several weeks or for a whole season. It was not unusual for the same members of the audience to come back night after night just to see the Cristianis perform their amazing tricks.

In 1933, a talent scout for America's biggest and most famous circus—Ringling Brothers and Barnum & Bailey—saw the Cristianis perform, and he asked them to come to the United States and join the Big Show, as it was (and still is) called. So the next year all the Cristianis packed up and got on a boat and came to America. They have been here ever since, and they have become American citizens. For almost a dozen years, the Cristianis performed with Ringling and with other, smaller shows that Ringling owned. At one time, the management of the Ringling show, which always moved from town to town in a long circus train, provided the Cristianis with their own private railroad car. On the side it said, in big letters, THE CRISTIANI FAMILY.

It was during the years with Ringling that the Cristianis —and particularly Lucio—became most famous. Audiences rose to their feet and applauded when they finished an act, and people all over the country knew that if they saw the Cristianis they would get more than their money's worth.

Lucio became so good at bareback riding that, a few years ago, he was admitted to the Circus Hall of Fame. When he received that honor, the operators of the Hall of Fame pointed out that Lucio had done two tricks on horseback that had never been done before (and that very few people have done since). One of them involved doing a full twist (in which the body is twisted completely around in the air) from the back of one moving horse to another.

The second, which was Lucio's greatest feat, was done with three horses running around the ring, one behind the other. Lucio was on the first horse, standing up. At the proper moment, he would jump up, do a full somersault in the air while the second horse was passing beneath him, and land on his feet on the back of the third horse. "Neither of these acts have been successfully performed on a regular basis by any other performer," said the Hall of Fame when Lucio was inducted into it in 1972.

In 1949, some of the Cristianis got the old itch to go out with their own show, and they went on the road with a circus that they half owned. It was called King Brothers–Cristiani Circus. Seven years later, they put on their very own show, the Cristiani Brothers Circus—a big, old-fashioned circus, with lots of elephants, a big tent, and trucks to move it from town to town. In addition to performing in it, Lucio was the circus's president.

Like his father and grandfather, Lucio was a real showman. He was daring. Once he took the whole show by truck to Alaska, where most of the natives had never seen a circus before. Thousands of Alaskans came to see it. There was a superstition among show people that any circus other than Ringling Brothers would not do well if it tried to set up a tent in Chicago. Lucio took the show to Chicago and put up the big white tent right next to Lake Michigan. It was a great success.

The Cristiani show lasted until 1961. It closed, says Lucio, because it had a bad season (that means it didn't make very much money) and because some of the members of the family weren't getting along well with some of the others. After 1961, the Cristiani brothers and sisters started going their own ways. One of them, Lucio's brother Pete, became a circus manager. Another brother became an elephant trainer. One started building rides for carnivals. Some retired from show business.

But Lucio stayed in the circus life. And sixteen years ago he had married his second wife, Gilda, who was a bareback rider with an Italian circus and who had come to the United States to perform. They continued going on the road, working for various circuses, from season to season. They took a little time off for Tino to be born. Then, three years later, Armando was born, on the road.

Gilda and Lucio Cristiani

4

ARMANDO'S TWO LIVES

With ancestors such as those, it would seem certain that Armando would *have* to be a performer. If being a circus person goes all the way back to your great-great-grandfather, and if you know that your family name practically *means* circus performer, then it must be hard to be something else.

But Armando's parents have been careful to let Armando know that his future belongs to him. If he wants to be an automobile salesman (as is his older brother Cris, who was born to Lucio and his first wife), then it is fine for him to be an automobile salesman. Of course, Lucio and Gilda would *like* to see Armando and Tino carry on the family name in the circus. "But we don't force them to be show people," said Lucio one time. "The thing is that I see *talent* in Armando and Tino. And I feel that through the life *I* had, I think they have an opportunity to have a good life and to be good entertainers. I guess in a few years they will probably decide, themselves, to do what they want to do. We're not going to force them."

If you ask Armando about all this, you'll get a pretty quick

Tino Cristiani

answer. Armando has decided already that he wants to be a circus performer. He likes the fact that he's a Cristiani. He likes the life of the circus (although sometimes he gets a little tired of it, and he finds himself yearning for the life of a normal eleven-year-old). He thinks he will be a performer for the rest of his life.

One thing that is on Armando Cristiani's mind almost all of the time when he's performing, and a lot of the time when he isn't, is the fact that he is not just a regular kid. He has a proud and famous name. And, because of that, he has to do his best.

"I want to be like my father," says Armando. "It's wonderful, having him for a father, because he's a great man and he'll always be a great man. It's easy, really, being a Cristiani, but it's also a lot of work. You have to be good. You can't be lazy. Sometimes my father tells me that I'm too lazy. And then I have to work harder to be good. If I'm going to be like my father, I've got to be very good."

Armando is not only a circus performer. He is also a youngster with the likes and dislikes most eleven-year-old boys have. He will tell you he likes hot dogs and baked beans a lot. He also likes bacon and scrambled eggs for breakfast, spaghetti, especially with garlic bread, steak, fish, pizza, peanuts, cauliflower, spinach, home-grown (only) tomatoes, and all kinds of soup.

"I like the food you buy at Burger Kings," says Armando. "I don't like the cold weather. I'm used to being in Florida, and it's hot there. I like fishing. I do salt-water fishing with a spin-casting rod. I catch big fish. I'm a good fisherman. Last year I made a fishing pole out of wood. I used some string and a hook and I baited it with some bread. And I caught a big giant catfish with it."

Armando may like to fish, but he doesn't like to hunt. "I don't like to kill all those animals," he says. He tried hunting once. He killed one rabbit and one bird. "I felt bad about it afterward," said Armando, "because I had taken their lives. Once in a while my friends at home in Florida will go hunting, but I don't like it. I like to start out with them, but after it starts I don't like it. I don't like to kill the animals."

Needless to say, Armando likes circus animals. "I like monkeys, and leopards, and gorillas," he says. "Gorillas are cute when they're babies. I like elephants a lot. We may get one someday. One of our leopards would ride on its back in the act. My family has owned sixteen elephants in the past. They had a really big elephant, about eleven feet tall. He had tusks that were seven feet long. He broke one tusk. They were too long, and one of them hit the ground while he was running, and it broke. They had to cut the other one to make it even.

"Myrtle's my favorite elephant on the Hoxie Brothers show. She's the leader of the herd. She's funny. She's the fattest thing here. She's the oldest one, too. She's sixty-four years old, I think. And that's old. But my father told me it doesn't matter how old you are. If you feel in good shape, you're okay."

Elephants, thank goodness, stay in good shape most of the time, but they do get sick. This happened to Myrtle and several of the other Hoxie Brothers elephants when the animals ate some bad hay and developed monstrous bellyaches. They almost died, and it took a visit from a local veterinarian to get them feeling good again.

There are some things that Armando doesn't know if he likes, because he hasn't been able to try them. Traveling and working make it hard to learn how to roller-skate, and living in a warm place like Florida makes it hard to learn to ski.

"I like to go to baseball games," says Armando. "What I *really* like best is football. My favorite team is the Miami Dolphins. I like football a lot because my cousin plays football." Tony Cristiani, who is the son of Lucio's brother Pete, is a professional player who used to play for the Dolphins. "Sometimes I feel bad because I can't play much myself," says Armando. "I might want to play in the Little League or something, but I can't because I travel. I like to look at books about baseball. It looks like fun."

Model airplanes that fly (Armando makes his own airplanes when he's at home in Florida during the wintertime) are also big on his list of favorite games. He likes checkers and chess, too, and all sorts of board games; but it's difficult to carry those games with him when the circus is on the road. The parts seem to get lost easily in the Cristianis' small trailer.

And Armando likes his minibike. He keeps the small motorcycle at his home in Sarasota, Florida. Armando's mother will not let him ride on the street. "She wants me to sell it," says Armando. "She's scared that it's dangerous. Because I've got to work, and if I break a leg that's trouble. If you have a broken leg, you can't face the public."

Armando loves the beach. Every summer, the Hoxie Brothers show spends a lot of time in New Jersey, along the beach, and the circus performers and bosses and workmen all try to take some time off in the afternoon and go to the ocean. Sometimes the beach is just a block or two away. Armando and Tino like to soak in the water and build fortresses in the sand and then finish up by covering themselves with wet sand and going into the water again.

But if you had to ask Armando where he liked best to go during the circus season, he would probably answer, "Shopping centers."

Most circus people like it when the show is playing near a shopping center because that means they can stock up on groceries, and they can do their laundry if there's a Laundromat nearby. And they, like everybody else, like to window-shop a little.

But for Armando a shopping center is a very special place. He likes to buy plastic models, and silly toys (like the sunglasses he once got that had battery-operated windshield

Armando's spare time:
He rests at a beach . . .

plays air hockey . . .

plays a pinball machine . . .

MONTGOMERY COUNTY FREE LIBRARY

INFORMATION · RECREATION · EDUCATION

visits a bookmobile . . .

waits for an order of pizza
while his friend Jerry hams it up.

wipers on them), and shirts. Armando likes T-shirts with funny words and pictures on them. He got one one time that had a big picture of a ketchup bottle on it. His favorite shirt was one that said ARMANDO across the back, but he lost it. After he lost it he felt bad for weeks.

Tino says Armando is a real fiend about shirts and pants that he especially likes. "He'll buy a shirt and he'll wear if for a month," says Armando's big brother. "When it gets dirty, he'll take a bucket of water and some soap and he'll wash it, without waiting for our mother to go to the laundry. Then he'll wait a couple of hours until it's dry and put it back on. He'll wear the same pair of pants until he gets tired of them, and then he'll switch to another favorite pair of pants. He keeps washing them. Sometimes he'll wash them at night, and in the morning, when it's time to move, they won't be dry. And Armando wants to wear them right away, so he'll hang them out the truck's window, while we're traveling, so they dry."

Armando is a great explorer. When the circus is playing next to a little stream, he likes that a lot because it means he can go exploring in the water. Once, when the show was next to a small stream in the North Carolina mountains, he told his mother to get ready to cook a big meal of crawfish for dinner because he was going to catch a lot. Armando searched in the stream for more than an hour, but he got only one, and he put that one back.

When there are big, tall trees on the circus lot, that is an invitation for Armando to do some climbing. It's hard *not* to climb trees when you're a member of a famous circus family that is known for its athletic ability. Armando could probably climb a tree and juggle at the same time if he wanted to.

When Armando goes into a shopping center and picks out

Tree climbing

a plastic Wolfman model or a new T-shirt, he's careful about spending his money because he knows it *is* his money. Armando doesn't get a regular allowance, the way some kids do. He gets paid for his work in the circus, and the money is his to spend any way he wants. Of course, his parents tell him to be careful and not to waste his hard-earned money, and most of the time Armando *is* careful.

Every week he gets paid $25 for his juggling act, $10 for his part in the trampoline act, and another $2 for helping with the leopards. At one point during his season with Hoxie Brothers, Armando had more than $700 saved up. To some people, that may sound like a very large amount of money for an eleven-year-old, but you have to remember something: a lot of circus performers work only six or seven months out of the year. There aren't many opportunities for them to work in the wintertime, and so they stay in Florida and live off their savings. Armando has to be careful not to use up all his savings, too, before the winter comes.

5

THE SECRETS OF SHOWMANSHIP

☆ ☆ ☆ ☆ ☆ ☆ ☆ ☆ ☆ ☆ ☆

One reason Cristianis are such good performers is that they have a long history of excellence behind them. It might be difficult for an average person to become convinced that it's possible to do a flip-flop on the back of a moving horse, but Cristianis know it can be done because they have relatives who can do it, and who can do it well.

Another reason is that there are very many Cristianis in show business, and for years they have been competing politely with each other, always trying to get better. So when Armando runs into the ring and starts his juggling act, it's almost as if his ancestors were looking over his shoulder and saying, "If you're a Cristiani, you have to do it better."

When the circus is on the road, you can see Armando practicing his juggling and trampoline work. But it's hard to practice bareback riding during the circus season, and so Armando does most of that practicing at home in Florida during the winter, when the family is not on the road.

The Cristianis live in Sarasota, where a lot of circus people make their homes. In the Cristianis' backyard there is a circus ring, just like the one in a real circus. Beside the ring are two tall poles connected by a cable in the air. A pulley hangs from the cable, and this is part of what is called, in the circus business, a *mechanic*. A mechanic is a device that keeps you from being hurt when you're learning new tricks. It works this way:

Armando puts on a very strong belt. Two ropes are attached to the belt, on the sides, and they go up in the air and through the pulley and down to the ground again. Armando gets on a horse and practices his tricks. Lucio or Gilda stands on the side telling him what he's doing right and what he's doing wrong, and also holding the free ends of the ropes. If Armando slips, the ropes hold him up and keep him from falling to the ground. One of his parents can gradually and safely lower him to the ground, and then he can start over again.

Armando also uses a mechanic when he's practicing new stunts on the trampoline. The Cristianis set up the trampoline in the backyard and hitch up the mechanic, and Armando and Tino try new tricks. The two boys have learned quickly on the trampoline, and they hardly ever need the mechanic now. "Last year," says Armando, "I started practicing the triple. I would bounce on the trampoline, and then go high and do three somersaults in the air and then land on Tino's shoulders. I tried and tried, and I missed it every time. Then all of a sudden I started doing it. Now it's easy for me."

And that's how you get to be very good at being a circus performer. You practice. Even if your last name is Cristiani, you practice. *Especially* if your last name is Cristiani, you practice. Armando has been a circus performer—on the trampoline—since he was three years old, and he still practices with Tino every day. He started practicing his juggling when he was seven years old, and he thinks he's only now getting to be a professional at it. Armando practiced four years with the balls and rings before he ever went in front of an audience. He has been working at his horsemanship since he was ten, and he still doesn't consider himself good enough to do any complicated bareback tricks before the public. But Armando keeps on practicing.

Practicing before an interested audience

One reason Armando learns so quickly is that he has a brother right there to work with. Tino is three years older than Armando, but he is a good brother, and he wants the act to work well. So he and Armando spend a lot of time working together to make themselves better.

"It's competition," says Tino. "But it's not jealousy. There's a lot of difference between competition and jealousy. We compete with each other a lot, but we're not jealous of each other. In competition, you learn a lot, and you have a lot of fun. You kid around, and you teach new tricks to each other. Last year I was hardly doing anything on the trampoline. I was doing the somersault and that's about all. But Armando and I practiced together, and that made us better."

"If we didn't practice together and compete when we're practicing," says Tino, "we wouldn't learn anything. What you do is you try a harder trick, and then the other one tries the harder trick, and that's the way you learn. That's the way my father learned. It was a big family, and people were always learning something from each other. You always try to outdo each other. That's the way you learn."

Besides, says Tino, Armando is a good person to be around. "He's a pretty good brother," he says. "Sometimes I get mad at him, and sometimes he gets mad at me, but I think we're like typical brothers. I wouldn't trade him in."

To do what Tino and Armando do, you don't have to be any special shape or size. You don't have to be superstrong or superbig. When Armando was eleven, he was four feet, eleven inches tall and he weighed seventy-five pounds. You *do* have to be in good physical condition, though, and that means that you have to eat the right kinds of food, get the right amount of rest, and get plenty of exercise. And practice.

"I've been practicing my juggling for four whole years," said Armando when he was with the Hoxie Brothers Circus. "And I can do five balls now. You start with two balls. Almost anybody can juggle two balls. It's better if they're small. You have to keep both of them in the air at the same time, crossing them all the time. And then, when you can do two well, you start trying three. That's the hard number. It's like throwing two balls, except that when you get two of them in the air, you have to throw the third one in the middle.

two . . .

One . . .

three . . .

four . . .

"When you do three balls, all of them are in the air at the same time. You practice that a lot, until you can do three balls well. I have a friend in Sarasota, named Scott, and he always watched me practicing at home, and he said he wanted to learn how to juggle. He practiced by himself for about a week, and then he could do three balls. One day he just did it, by himself, without me telling him how to do it.

You get a few balls in the air,
and maybe you drop some . . .

and you pick them up . . .

. . . and start all over again.

"When you can do three well," said Armando, "you go to four. And you keep on going like that. I can do five balls now. That's hard to do, but if you practice it, it's not too hard. But you have to practice all the time. Someday I'm going to be able to do seven."

Armando means it when he says you have to practice all the time. When he was traveling with the Hoxie show, Armando could be seen juggling for hours each day. Sometimes, the Cristianis would pull their trailer into a new lot, and as soon as the animals were unloaded Armando would be outside with his balls and rings, practicing, next to the trailer. Sometimes he would be walking through the Big Top without his equipment, before a performance, and he would pick up three little rocks from the ground and start juggling them as he walked. "Practice, practice, practice," said Armando. "That's the key to the whole thing. I practiced one time so much that I made a sore on my hand, from catching the rings. Sometimes my mother says I practice too much. I usually practice about four hours a day, and that's too much. But I want to keep getting better."

When Armando talks about "getting better," he doesn't necessarily mean that he wants to be able to juggle more and more balls and rings. There are some jugglers, he says, who can keep as many as eleven objects going in the air at once. Everybody thinks of these people as great jugglers, but Armando says there's something else that is just as important as being able to juggle a lot of things.

"In a good juggling act," he says, "it doesn't really matter how many rings or balls you do. It's *how* you do it. What I mean is, if you do six rings and you're always dropping them, that means you don't know how to do it well. If you can just do five and you can do those five *well*, then that's better than

Examining a hand
made sore by practicing

doing six *not* so well. I don't think the people in the audience really count to see how many balls or rings you're doing. They're interested in how *well* you do it. And if you're going to do something, you might as well do it right."

There was one circus performer, says Armando, who could juggle a fantastic number of balls and do it well at the same time. Armando would like someday to be as good as this performer.

"His name was Enrico Rastelli," said Armando. "My father knew him many years ago." Lucio met Rastelli in

1941, when both were working for a famous circus in Paris. They became great friends. Rastelli died of leukemia when he was still a young man, and Armando never got to see him perform.

Rastelli could juggle as many as ten balls at once. He could keep eight plates in the air. And he used to juggle six plates in his hands while he kept a ball bouncing on his head. But that wasn't all: at the same time, Rastelli was skipping a rope with one of his feet and using the other leg to spin a ring. "I don't think there'll ever be another person like him," Lucio once said.

"Rastelli had it all," said Armando. "He could juggle a lot of things, and he could do it well. But it was more important that he did it *well*."

What Armando was talking about was what circus people mean when they talk about *showmanship*. Showmanship means doing your best, and it also means letting the audience sort of feel your excitement and your talent at work in front of them. It's a very hard thing to define. Circus people always get a little tongue-tied when they talk about it. But everybody agrees that Cristianis in general have a great deal of showmanship and that Armando has inherited and learned a lot of it already.

Showmanship not only means doing your best before the audience; it also means admitting a mistake if you make one and trying again to do it right. Sometimes, for example, when the Cristianis are doing the "three-high" on the trampoline, Armando doesn't make it all the way to the top of his brother's shoulders. So he tries again until he does. The audience appreciates this because it sees how really difficult the trick is.

"Another thing about showmanship," says Armando, "is how you act on your way going into the ring and coming out of it. And how you take your bows. You don't just walk into the ring to start your act. You *run.* And you start juggling right away, and you let the people know that you like your work. And when you finish, you take a nice bow. My mother keeps saying, 'Always take a good bow and smile.' Personality counts a lot."

Sometimes, says Armando, you have to smile when you don't at all feel like smiling. That, too, is part of showmanship. "Sometimes you feel bad that day," he says, "and sometimes you just don't feel like working. Sometimes you have a stomach ache or a headache. And sometimes you just have a bad day.

"But you have to do it anyway, because you're in show business. When you're in show business, you have to work if you're going to get paid for it. A lot of people have paid their money to see you perform, and you want to give them their money's worth. You want that even if you feel bad that day, or even if it's raining and you had to walk through a lot of mud to get to the Big Top."

And what happens on a *good* day?

"I just feel normal when I'm in the ring working," says Armando. "I don't feel nervous. Well, *sometimes* I feel a little nervous, when there are a lot of people watching or when I know some other performers are visiting the show and they're watching me. But mostly I just feel normal, and the reason for that is that it's easy work for me. It's easy because I've been practicing it such a long time.

"And after it's over I feel tired and sweaty. And I'm thinking about my good old trailer and how I can lie down after I work. And I'm thinking about that good dinner my mother's making for me."

Practice, practice, practice

6

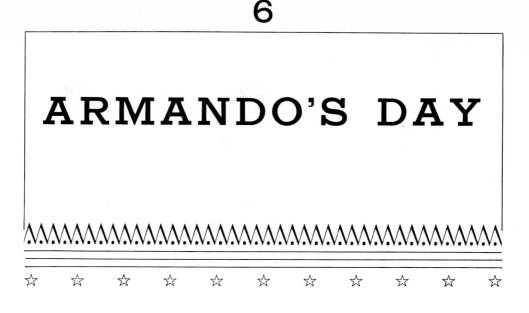

ARMANDO'S DAY

☆ ☆ ☆ ☆ ☆ ☆ ☆ ☆ ☆ ☆ ☆

One morning, Armando woke up in the trailer in the center of an empty field in Crawfordsville, Indiana. It was in the middle of June, and the circus was slowly but surely moving eastward. The next town would be Shelbyville. The circus trucks had left before dawn.

When you looked at the Cristiani trailer from the outside, it seemed quite large. It was thirty-six feet long and eight feet wide, and it was pulled by a truck-tractor. If you had to live in it for seven months, though, it would seem very small. Only the front half of the trailer was used for the Cristianis' living quarters. The rear was used to carry the horses, the leopards, the folded-up trampoline, and all sorts of other props.

When Armando woke up this particular morning, he climbed out of his bed—it was a small compartment that he shared with Tino in the front end of the trailer—and walked a few feet through the trailer to the small bathroom. He brushed his teeth. Then he went into the little room that served as the kitchen, dining room, and living room. He sat down at the table (at night it folded up and its seats became a bed for Armando's parents), and he had a cup of coffee.

The Cristiani trailer parked on a circus lot in Indiana under a threatening sky

Then Armando helped bring the horses in. Usually in mild or warm weather they were left outside overnight. Armando, Tino, and Lucio brought the animals in and carefully packed them into the rear of the trailer. They had to make sure that none of the cages or props would roll around while the family was traveling.

Then there was breakfast. Gilda fixed scrambled eggs and bacon. After that, the family all climbed into the cab of the truck and set out for Shelbyville. Gilda and Lucio sat in the front, and Armando and Tino crawled into a small compartment behind the seats.

Armando sits on his "front porch"

At home inside the trailer: in the kitchen . . . and in the sleeping compartment he shares with Tino

By the time the Cristianis were pulling away from the lot, the trucks that belonged to the circus—the ones that carried the tent, the seats, the elephants, and the other equipment—had already arrived in Shelbyville. One of the circus employees had driven during the night to the new town, and he had put little cardboard arrows on telephone poles and road signs along the way. Each circus has its own distinctive arrow, and the one for Hoxie Brothers looks like an H with an arrow point on the top. It is purple.

The arrows show the circus people the correct route from one town to the next. The next town could be anything from four miles to more than one hundred miles away, but the average distance, on the Hoxie Brothers show, was about thirty-five miles. On this day, Shelbyville was a medium jump, about sixty-five miles. It was almost all on good, flat highways.

The Hoxie Brothers Circus moves all over the eastern part of the United States. The season starts in early spring and ends in midfall. The show goes from Florida through Georgia, South Carolina, North Carolina, Virginia, West Virginia, Ohio, Indiana, Michigan, Wisconsin, Pennsylvania, New Jersey, Maryland, and Delaware, before heading back to Florida in October.

That's a pretty heavy schedule, and the circus covers it by staying, usually, only one day in each town. Early each morning, the circus trucks arrive in a new town, and the workmen set up the tent. They put the seats inside the tent, along with all the performers' riggings and props. That night, the big tent comes down, the elephants are put away for the night, and everybody goes to sleep. Early the next morning, the circus moves again, to a new town, and it starts all over again.

The big, important circus acts—such as the Cristianis—

Hoxie Brothers Circus arrows show the way.

do not work for the same circus season after season. They like to work for many different circuses, and the shows themselves don't want to bring the same feature acts back to the same towns year after year. So Armando and his parents have followed many circus arrows all over the United States. "Once, when we were on another show," says Armando, "we had a real long jump, from California to Boston. It was three thousand, five hundred miles. It took us about five days. I really got tired of traveling then."

On the ride to Shelbyville, Armando and Tino helped their father look for the arrows. Everything went well, and the arrows took the family directly onto the new circus lot. Sometimes, though, there are problems. Flat tires are among the most common difficulties, and changing a tire on a heavy truck or trailer is a lot harder than changing one on an automobile. "And we always seem to have trouble when we drive through the mountains," says Armando. "There's almost always some kind of breakdown."

For that reason, circus people seem less happy when they have to cross over mountains, no matter how pretty the scenery might be. If they have a breakdown and don't get to the next lot in time, they won't be able to perform. That's why circus people have to become pretty good mechanics. And there's an old saying in show business that is just as important now as it ever was: *the show must go on.*

By the time the Cristianis and the other performers had arrived in Shelbyville, the circus workmen had put up the Big Top's huge centerpole, which was fifty-five feet tall, and they were starting to haul the heavy canvas tent up the pole. The side-show tent, where most of the show's animals stayed, was up, and the elephants were out of their truck and helping to move things around.

Someone had already decided where the main entrance of the circus would be. Halfway around the tent from the main entrance was the back door.

Lucio drove the truck as close as possible to the back door. He parked, and Armando glanced around, getting his first look at the new lot. Sometimes the lot is way out in the country, with farmland all around it. Sometimes it's in town but in a not very pretty part of town. Sometimes it's in a nice public park. Sometimes (and best of all, thinks Armando) it is at or near a shopping center.

In Shelbyville, the lot was sort of halfway in town and halfway out, at a county fairgrounds. There were no shopping centers nearby, but it was a pretty lot, with a racetrack for horses next door and lots of fine old trees, just right for climbing. On the racetrack, harness drivers trained their horses for a race that would be held a few days later.

Once they were settled on the new lot, the family started getting ready for the day's work. Armando and Tino helped Lucio unload the animals. The horses were tied outside, where they could be close to their feed and water. The leopard cages were slowly rolled down a ramp from the truck to the ground, and the trampoline came out, too.

Gilda straightened up inside the trailer and got some things together for lunch. The Cristianis eat only light meals during the day. They prefer to go to work at night on empty stomachs. When the show is all over, they can count on a big, tasty meal from Gilda's kitchen.

Usually, at about this time, some people from the town, including kids who are Armando's age, will start walking through the backyard. It is an old tradition for folks from town to come out and watch the show going up on circus day.

Almost always the town people walk over to see the Cristiani leopards. They are beautiful animals, and most people
don't have a chance to see a leopard very often. A member of
the family, often Armando, has to be stationed outside to warn
people not to get too close to the cats.

Sure enough, some town people did come to the lot in
Shelbyville, and they came to see the leopards. Armando
had to explain several times that the leopards were dangerous.
But at the same time he sat on their cage and put his fingers
inside and scratched the leopards' necks. "It's O.K. for *me* to
touch them," he explained to the town people. "They know
me." But Armando was careful anyway.

By early afternoon, most of the circus people had
finished their move to the new town. They took it easy for a
while. Some of them took naps, and some watched television
or listened to the radio. Some took their dirty clothes to a
laundry. But the Cristianis are different. For them, afternoon
is the time to practice.

Armando went into the trailer and came out with five
balls—the kind anyone can buy in a dime store. He practiced
juggling. When he finished with the balls, he practiced with
the rings.

His mother, in the meantime, got the baby leopard out
of her cage and took her walking. So far, only the grown
leopards had been used in the family's act. But Gilda hoped
that the baby leopard could be taught a part in the act. Gilda
knew that one of the first things she had to do was to get the
baby accustomed to being out of her cage and to being in
front of humans. So Gilda went walking with the leopard on
a leash. The town people always did double takes when they
saw this.

"They are beautiful animals . . ."

The leopards are quite dangerous. A lot of town people think that, since the cats live in the same trailer with the Cristianis and since they perform without cages, they must be tame. They are not. Every once in a while, if you get too close to their cage or if you come too close to the baby when she's being walked, you will see that jungle cats are never really tame. They jump at you, and sometimes they try to bite you. Armando has been bitten a few times.

"One time one of them was licking my finger," says Armando. "She was in the cage, and I had my finger inside the cage, and she just grabbed it and pulled the skin off. It didn't feel good at all. Sometimes they jump on me when they get the chance. I think they like to do that because they know I'm smaller."

The leopards have been with the Cristianis so long, though, that most of the time Gilda and Lucio and Tino and Armando can get close enough to scratch their necks. Gilda is particularly friendly with the cats. In her act with them, she rewards them not with pieces of sugar, but with kisses.

There's almost always a little time left over after the afternoon practicing, and Tino and Armando usually spend some of it playing. If it's a nice, smooth lot, they may take turns riding Tino's new ten-speed bike. If there are trees around, as there were this day in Shelbyville, they may go tree climbing.

One summer day in Pennsylvania, they found a shopping center with a whole roomful of pinball machines and air hockey, and they spent most of their afternoon (and a lot of their money) there.

Gilda walking the baby leopard, with a town kid watching

And then, before you know it, it's time to go to work. You can tell the difference by the town people. They may have been on the lot all day, just strolling around, but at about five-thirty you always see some of them walking up the midway toward the ticket wagon, and you know they're there to see the show. Armando saw the people beginning to arrive in Shelbyville, and he saw that the sun was getting low in the sky, and he headed back to the trailer and started getting ready for work.

That meant, for one thing, that Armando had to get clean. There's a complete bathroom in the Cristiani trailer, but there's also a complete family of Cristianis who need to use it, all at once, just before the show. And water, in the circus, is a precious item. Once a day, an employee of the circus comes by with a big water truck and pumps water into the tanks of the performers' trailers, but it seems as if there's never enough water for everyone. So Armando often gets a bucket, fills it from the water truck, and uses it to wash at least part of his body.

Then come the costumes. Gilda and Lucio decide, each day, which of their costumes the family will wear, and shortly before show time each Cristiani gets dressed in his or her costume. On this day, Armando put on his bright red bell-bottom pants that his mother had made, along with a ruffled white shirt and a red jacket. And then he combed his hair and went outside and practiced with his juggling rings because he knew that before long Phil Chandler would be blowing his whistle and calling, "Fifteen minutes!"

"What a lot of kids don't understand," says Armando, "is they think that being with the circus is all play. I work!"

Taking a bucket bath

7

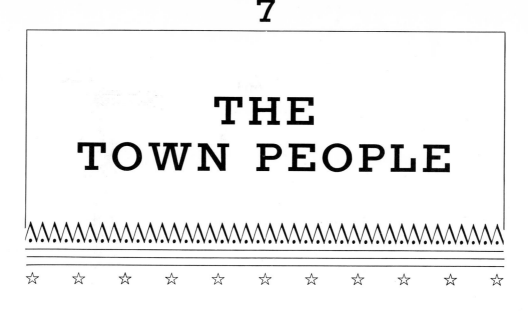

THE TOWN PEOPLE

Because Phil Chandler is the ringmaster for the circus, he's the fellow who, after almost every performance, gets someone from the audience who walks up to him and asks a question or two. A good percentage of the questions are about Armando. And Phil says that the question he gets asked most often is about Armando's education. "People want to know what he does about school," says Phil.

Armando and Tino do not go to regular schools. They don't sit in a classroom, and they don't see the teacher write things on the blackboard. In fact, they don't even *have* a teacher. But that doesn't mean that they don't get an education. They do their schoolwork by mail.

Armando takes a correspondence course with the Calvert School in Baltimore. The school specializes in teaching children who can't go to regular schools. Some of the students are sick and must stay home. Some of them are in show business, like Armando, and are on the road during part or all of the regular school year.

Every few weeks, the Calvert School sends Armando a big envelope full of books and papers. It mails the envelopes

Doing schoolwork on top of the leopard cage

to one of Armando's relatives, who knows where the circus will be playing and who sends them along to Armando.

Some kids like to talk about how they would just as soon not have to go to school, but they probably would miss it if it weren't there. Armando feels this way about his correspondence course. When an envelope is late in coming, he worries about it. Armando likes to learn. He figures that the world will be more interesting to him if he knows more about it.

In the almost seven months that Armando spent with Hoxie Brothers Circus, he received quite a few envelopes from Baltimore. There were folders with arithmetic exercises in them, and there were short stories to read, and there were thick books. With each mailing there was a test. Armando did his reading and his exercises, and then he took the test. Then he mailed the test back to the school, and someone there checked Armando's work, just as a teacher in a regular school grades the tests that the students take. Armando usually did well on his tests.

There is another source of education for Armando, and that is his mother and father. Neither of them has a great deal of formal education, the kind one gets by going to a college or university, but they both have a lot of *informal* education. When the Cristiani family gathers around the table for that big meal at the end of the day, food is not all that they get. They also talk about what has happened in the world and in the nation, and Armando learns a lot more by listening and asking questions. Lucio Cristiani speaks six languages, including Latin, and it is difficult to finish dinner in the Cristiani trailer without feeling well fed *and* well educated.

A lot of circus people think they've got the best lives in the world, despite the occasional mud and rain and bad days.

They're in the out-of-doors most of the time, and they do a lot of traveling, and they get to see lots of different parts of the country. If they're in a place today that they don't particularly like, they know that tomorrow they'll be in a different place and they might like *that* one.

But circus people wouldn't be able to make their livings if it weren't for the people who buy tickets and come to see them perform. Some circus performers refer to the people in their audiences as "towners," and when they say that, it doesn't sound like a completely friendly term. It's not a *mean* word; it's not the most friendly word, either. But performers who were born on the circus, like Armando, know that there could be no circus without the audiences, and they are glad to see the town people.

In almost every town that the circus plays, kids come into the backyard to see Armando. They don't know him, but they know he's a kid, too, and they know that he works with the circus. The ones who are shy hang around a few yards away from Armando and watch him practice or feed and pet the leopards, and they don't say very much. As often as not, when Armando sees a kid who's shy he walks up to the kid himself and starts a conversation.

Some of the visitors are not shy. They walk right up to Armando and start asking him questions about how it is to be a circus boy.

"In almost every town we come to," says Armando, "some kids from the town come into the backyard and ask me questions. They ask me how it is living with the circus and all that. I tell them it's a little different from where they live, in a house. They've got a nice bathroom and television and all that, and they have time to relax. And I don't have all those things.

"I also tell them that I have to work every day, and with-

Armando talking with a town boy

out a day off, usually. I tell them that I have to work on Sundays, too. I always tell them that because a lot of them think I have such a great life, and I have to let them know that it's a lot of work, too.

"Then they ask me is it hard to work on the trampoline, and I tell them that it takes practice. I tell them that it took me four years to practice the juggling.

"And they always ask me how I got on the circus. And I tell them I was born on the circus.

"Sometimes they ask me if I'm *glad* I was born on the circus. I tell them, yes, I'm glad because it's fun to travel around. Once in a while it gets boring, though, you know, and you want to go home because you do the same things over and over every day. You get tired. And you have to work hard. I always tell them that. And they never say anything when I tell them that. They think that if *they* were in the circus, it'd never be boring for them. But that's because they don't have to do any of the work that goes with being in the circus.

"Sometimes I ask them questions, too," says Armando. "I ask them what they do all day, and which sports they like, and things like that. Sometimes I think their lives are very interesting, the same way they think my life is interesting. I'm not jealous of them, and I don't think they're jealous of me. We each have good things that we do.

"I get to work with the circus, but they get to play a lot of games and go to football and baseball games and things like that, and I don't get to do that. Sometimes I like the idea of going to a regular school, and not having to work and practice all the time, and having lots of friends who live nearby."

Often the town kids who come to visit are girls, and Armando especially likes that. Armando likes girls a lot. Sometimes, when he knows a town girl is watching him practice his juggling, he juggles harder and faster.

Once a town girl came to the trailer after a performance, and she knocked on the door. Gilda answered it. The girl asked if she could see the boy who did the juggling. She said she wanted to kiss him. Gilda invited the girl in, and she saw Armando and gave him a big kiss. Armando blushed a little, but he enjoyed it.

Every once in a while, a town kid (or, more often, a group of town kids) will come on the lot, before or after a performance, and he will be jealous of Armando and Tino and other circus kids. Sometimes the jealous kids will stand around and make mean comments about the circus kids, and sometimes they'll throw things. Sometimes they'll even pick a fight. Anybody who picks a fight with Armando should know something first: Cristianis stick together.

Because some people don't like to see other people succeed, they pick on the people who do. When the Cristiani family came to work in the United States, in the 1930s, they were a big success. And every now and then someone would come to the lot and start a fight with one of the Cristiani men. The rule then was that if one Cristiani was attacked, all the others thought of it as *their* fight, too. So all the Cristiani men would start fighting. There was a good reason for this: if one of the Cristianis was hurt in a fight, he couldn't work. And if he couldn't work, the family's act would suffer.

The same rule applies today. If somebody picks on Armando, all Armando has to do is yell, and Tino will appear. And if Tino needs help, Lucio will arrive. The Cristianis individually are quite strong, and they're a lot stronger when they are together.

Once, during the season with the Hoxie show, some teen-agers in New Jersey started a fight with Tino. Tino had said "hello" to a town girl, and the teen-agers didn't like that. Before it was over, Armando and Lucio were in the fight, and the attackers were running away as fast as they could. The Cristianis would rather not have to fight at all. They are peace-loving people. But if someone threatens one of them, he threatens all of them. It's far better, think the Cristianis, for nobody to threaten anybody. "It's wrong to be jealous of people," says Armando. "It's better to be friends."

8

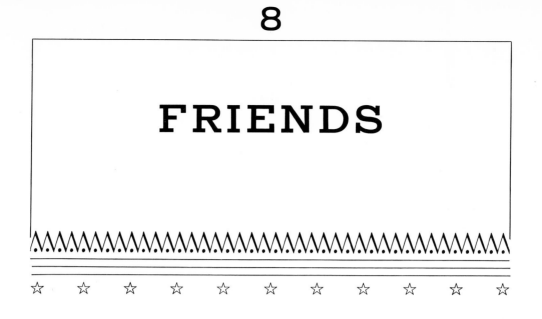

FRIENDS

A kid like Armando, who doesn't like jealousy and who welcomes the curiosity of town kids, has a lot of friends. Armando has friends back in Sarasota, kids from his neighborhood, and when he's in the middle of a circus season, he thinks about them and misses them. He has friends on the circus, too, although these friendships usually last just a season.

He also has a friend back in Sarasota who's a friend on the circus, too. That's Jerry Walker, the son of Alice and Johnny Walker, who operate the food wagon on the Hoxie Brothers show. The Walkers live just half a mile from the Cristianis in Sarasota.

Jerry goes to regular school in Florida, and so Armando doesn't see him until the summer begins. Then Jerry comes to live with his father and mother on the show, and he and Armando play whenever Armando isn't working or practicing. One of the toys they liked best, a few years ago, was smash-up derby cars. These are plastic cars with spring motors. You wind two of them up and point them at each other. When they crash together, they fly apart. But it's all right; you can put them back together easily.

Armando made another special friend when he was on the Hoxie Brothers Circus. Her name was Robin Anne Chandler, and she was the daughter of the ringmaster. Robin Anne had long blond hair, the same color as Armando's. She was Armando's age, and she and Armando were very good friends.

"I like her a lot," said Armando one time. "She's a good friend. She's very cute. You might even say I love her."

After Robin Anne had been with the show awhile, she started helping her father in his magic act. Robin Anne got a nice costume, and she helped her father make her mother float on air and do other tricks. Later, Robin Anne started helping Armando with his juggling. She stood by the side of the ring and handed him his props. It was likely that in a year or so Robin Anne might start learning her own act, so that she could be a circus performer, too.

Armando and Robin Anne stayed friends all that summer, but there came a time when Robin Anne had to go back to her home, in Dayton, Ohio, and back to school. Jerry left, too, and suddenly Armando didn't have many friends his own age left on the circus. And that's when he started thinking seriously about home, too.

9

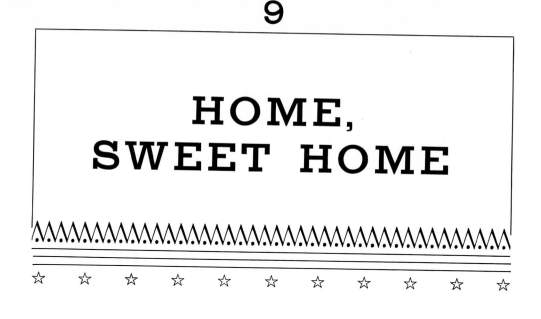

HOME, SWEET HOME

"Sometimes I get lonely," said Armando as the season neared its end. It was September, and Jerry and Robin Anne had left the circus and returned to their homes and to school. There weren't many people for Armando to play with. There weren't even many town kids who came on the lot because they were in school during the day, too.

"I was lonely when Jerry left, and I was lonely when Robin Anne left," he said. "I had nothing to do. Right now I don't have anybody to play with. But the season's almost over, and we're going home pretty soon.

"And today I'm just thinking of home, sweet home. I'll get up in the morning and watch color television and just lie around, and at night instead of working I can just lie on the couch and take it easy. And I have my minibike and my toys and everything. The first day you're home after a season, it's weird. You go around, and you feel like you just came home from seeing a circus! You get home, and you unload everything, and you go to sleep, and then when you get up in the morning, everything looks different from the way it looked for the past seven months. I always ride around on my bike looking at things. It's weird.

"But after a while you start getting used to it again. You see all your friends, and you go to the movies, and I always invite my friends over to dinner not long after I get home."

The season with Hoxie Brothers came to an end on a Saturday night in early October, in Valdosta, Georgia. Although it was fall, it was very warm. That part of Georgia is just a few miles from the Florida state line, and it would not get really cold at all during the fall and winter. On the last day, Jerry Walker came to visit the show, with his older brothers and sisters. He and Armando put up a large plastic swimming pool in front of the Big Top, and they played and splashed in it for several hours, until it was time for Armando to get ready for his last day of work.

That night Armando carried his banner through Spec, and he worked on the trampoline with his father and brother, and he worked in the horse act, and he did his juggling, and he did it all very well. It looked as if he were a better juggler than he had been at the beginning of the season.

And then, at about nine-thirty on that Saturday night, the season ended. The performers stood around in the backyard after it was all over, and the workmen started taking out the seats and props, and everybody said good-bye.

The Chandlers hitched up their trailer. Early the next morning they would leave for Ohio. Ruben and Magaly Rosales had many more miles to cover—they had to go to Mexico before they would be home. The tent, and the props, and the elephants and other animals, and the big trucks that

Armando and Jerry Walker in the pool at Valdosta

carried the seats and poles and props—all these things be-longed to the circus itself, and they would travel to a place in Florida, out behind some orange groves, to spend the next few months. It was called *winter quarters*. For the circus people, the winter was now starting.

"It's sad," said Armando. "You know that you're going to miss your friends. You're going to miss the audiences, too, but mostly it's your friends. It's always after the last show that you feel most sad. You have to say good-bye and everything. Sometimes people cry at the end." Armando was not crying as he said this, but he looked very sad.

The next morning, the Cristianis loaded up their trailer for the last time and drove to Sarasota. It took them more than half a day to get there, but they didn't mind because they knew they were finally going home. And they knew that when they got back home, they could take it easy for a while. The Cristianis liked their work (you could tell that by watching them perform), but they needed a rest. They had been doing their work twice a day, sometimes three times, usually every day of the week, for almost seven months, and now it was time for a little relaxation.

The Cristiani house was one story tall, made out of concrete blocks, and it was on the edge of Sarasota. There was a big field behind the house, and in it was a barn, for the horses and the leopards, that Lucio and Armando and Tino and their uncle had built. Right behind the house was the circus ring that they used for practicing. Now there were weeds growing in the ring because it had not been used for more than half a year. After a few weeks of resting the Cristianis would start practicing again, and the weeds would disappear.

Armando was looking very sad.

There were palm trees around the house. Inside, there were two bedrooms, one for Lucio and Gilda and the other for Armando and Tino. There was a big living room, with a painting of a circus performer, and a big playroom, and a sunroom with plenty of windows that let in the light. There were lots of scrapbooks that the Cristianis kept. In a day or two, Armando would go through the trailer and find some newspaper clippings to add to the scrapbooks. Several times during the season newspaper reporters had come to the circus and had written stories about Armando.

The Cristianis opened up the windows and let the fresh air in, and slowly the house came alive again. They took turns taking baths in the full-sized bathroom, and then they all ate a meal cooked on the full-sized stove. They sat at a full-sized table while they were eating, and it felt good for a change. Then they went to bed early because they were tired.

Armando slept until ten o'clock the next morning. He could have slept a lot longer because he was tired, but he was too excited about being home again, and there were things he wanted to do. That night the family would go to dinner at the home of his grandmother, Emma Cristiani, the trapeze star who had helped to build the famous circus family. And there were things to do before that.

After breakfast Armando helped clean up the yard. The first thing he checked on was his cactus. Just before the family had gone out with the circus in March, Armando had found a tiny cactus lying in the yard. No one knew where it had come from. Armando had carefully picked it up and planted it next to the house and watered it, and then he had left it there all summer. Now the cactus had grown big and strong, and Armando was happy to see it again.

Armando went to his room and did a little schoolwork.

It was a nice bedroom, full of musical instruments and plastic models that Armando and Tino had made. There was a desk, and bookshelves full of books, and a poster that said LOVE AND PEACE, and, next to the poster, a black light that made the poster glow in exciting colors. And there were circus posters on the wall.

Then it was afternoon, and Armando was glad because that meant that his friends would be getting out of school and coming to see him. Before long they arrived: Scott, who had been Armando's close friend for five years, and Randy, and Chris, and Eric, and Marty. Armando got out his minibike and rode around the yard some, and the boys tumbled in the backyard, and they asked Armando how the season had been.

Scott said, "How did you do in the circus?"

"I did well," said Armando. "Everything went fine. But I'm glad to get home."

"How were the leopards?" asked Scott.

"They really did good," said Armando. "In the last few days we put the baby leopard in the act, and she did just like she'd been performing all her life."

"How'd you do on your juggling?" asked Scott.

"I did real good," said Armando. "How'd *you* do on *your* juggling?" Armando had taught Scott how to juggle, and now Scott knew how to keep three balls in the air at once.

"I still know how to juggle," said Scott. "You're a good teacher."

"All it takes is practice," said Armando. "The best juggler in the world was Rastelli. That's what my father says."

"I thought the best juggler in the world was named Armando," said Scott. He was smiling.

"No," said Armando. He was smiling, too. "You can't say that yet."

Armando at home in Florida:
in front of his home . . .

on his minibike . . .

in his room playing the guitar . . .

with his grandmother, the former trapeze artist